Zeze

omenicia

This is the official holy book of the religion Ommeism. This holds pieces of the omenic language and shares the stories and beliefs of Ommeism.

Este es el libro sagrado oficial de la religión Ommeísmo. Contiene fragmentos del lenguaje oménico y comparte las historias y creencias del ommeísmo.

此宗教之官方也圣书　Ommeism.　含 omenic 言之片段,分 Ommeism 之信。

هذا هو الكتاب المقدس الرسمي للدين Ommeism. هذا يحمل أجزاء من اللغة الomenic ويشارك قصص ومعتقدات Ommeism

यह धर्म ओमेवाद की आधिकारिक पवित्र पुस्तक है। यह ओमेनिक भाषा के टुकड़े रखता है और ओमेवाद की कहानियों और विश्वासों को साझा करता है। .

Dies ist das offizielle heilige Buch der Religion Ommeism. Dies enthält Teile der omenischen Sprache und teilt die Geschichten und Überzeugungen des Ommeismus.

係宗教嘅官方聖書Ommeism. 它包含咗omenic語言嘅片段, 並分享咗Ommeism嘅故仔同信仰。

C'est le livre saint officiel de la religion Omméisme. Celui-ci contient des morceaux de la langue omenique et partage les histoires et les croyances de l'omméisme.

זהו הספר הקדוש הרשמי של דת האומיזם. זה מחזיק חלקים של השפה האומית וחולק את הסיפורים והאמונות של האומיזם.

Это официальная священная книга религии Оммеизм. Он содержит фрагменты зловещего языка и делится историями и верованиями Оммеизма.

Este é o livro sagrado oficial da religião Ommeísmo. Este contém pedaços da linguagem omênica e compartilha as histórias e crenças do ommeísmo.

The Fates

In the genesis of existence, there existed naught but a solitary star suspended in the vast expanse of nothingness. This radiant celestial body was the guardian of a divine being known as Attonatona, a luminous goddess whose brilliance illuminated the void. Yet, despite her radiant splendor, Attonatona began to wane, her once resplendent form gradually fading into the darkness.

In a desperate bid for preservation, Attonatona shattered fragments of her essence, birthing two sons—Feai'ka and Atomaseseai—to govern over the desolate expanse. Together, the brothers fashioned the raw elements of the void into minute particles known as allois, entrusting Feai'ka, the arbiter of fate, with their manipulation and experimentation.

Thus began the cosmic dance of creation, as Feai'ka and Atomaseseai crafted myriad planets, each imbued with its own unique essence and character. Unbeknownst to them, their creative fervor inadvertently birthed a second star, its incandescent radiance illuminating the cosmos. From its fiery embrace emerged Heaia, a goddess of unparalleled beauty and grace, whose heart would soon intertwine with Feai'ka's in an eternal bond.

As a testament to their love, Feai'ka orchestrated a cosmic spectacle, orchestrating the collision of two celestial bodies to birth their progeny. From the wreckage emerged a daughter, destined to embody the union of their divine essences.

Meanwhile, the surviving planet bore witness to the meticulous craftsmanship of Atomaseseai, who adorned its barren surface with layers of geological splendor. This once desolate world transformed into a realm of arid deserts and towering mountains, reminiscent of the celestial bodies that adorned the heavens.

Intrigued by his brother's handiwork, Atomaseseai descended upon the planet, where he encountered Maheai'ja, a goddess on the brink of oblivion. Moved by her plight, Atomaseseai bestowed upon her a gift of life-sustaining liquid, Quati, and a daughter named Quatica, whose aquatic form shimmered with ethereal beauty.

As Quatica flourished under Maheai'ja's nurturing gaze, she formed a bond with Annimkamakai, Maheai'ja's daughter, and together they reveled in the wonders of their burgeoning world. Yet, their idyllic existence was soon disrupted by the arrival of twin siblings, Grazzer and Heai Grazzer, whose boundless ambition sparked a rivalry that would shape the destiny of their realm.

Driven by their creative fervor, Grazzer and Heai Grazzer embarked on a competition of divine craftsmanship, each vying to surpass the other's feats of ingenuity. With a single gesture, Grazzer summoned forth towering mountains that pierced the heavens, while Heai Grazzer wielded the elements to conjure bolts of lightning that ignited the skies.

Yet, from the ashes of their rivalry emerged a sinister force, a primordial flame known as Herinkeai, whose voracious hunger consumed all light in its path. From its fiery depths arose Herika, a timid spirit who recoiled from the presence of others, particularly Quatica, whose serene countenance stirred feelings of unease within her.

As the gods' creations flourished and evolved, new forms of life emerged from the depths of the oceans, propelled by Annimkamakai's boundless creativity. Witnessing their ascent to the surface, Annimkamakai decreed the need for terrestrial rulers to maintain balance and order.

Thus, from the primordial mists descended Quati, a life-giving essence that cascaded from the heavens, heralding the arrival of Mink, a goddess whose benevolent gaze ushered in an era of prosperity and abundance. With her arrival, life flourished like never before, as she gifted the gods with rain and sustenance, ensuring the continued vitality of their creation.

Meanwhile, Annimkamakai, inspired by the evolving tapestry of life, crafted creatures in her own image—beings she dubbed Hinkis, the progenitors of a species destined to walk the earth as stewards of their realm. And thus, amidst the celestial symphony of creation, the intricate web of existence continued to unfold, guided by the hands of divine beings whose influence shaped the very fabric of reality itself

The First Hinkis

In the infancy of human existence, amidst the rugged landscapes of the primordial earth, three figures emerged from the mists of time—Lakleai, Truzie, and Helono, the first of the Hinkis. Together, they traversed the untamed wilderness, forging bonds of camaraderie amidst the harsh realities of survival.

Truzie and Lakleai, their spirits intertwined like the roots of ancient trees, shared a deep connection that transcended the bounds of mere friendship. Their laughter echoed through the valleys as they embarked on daring adventures, hunting elusive prey and braving the unforgiving elements of their arid homeland.

Yet, amidst the laughter and camaraderie, a shadow loomed over Helono, whose heart harbored a love unrequited. Despite his silent yearning for Lakleai, he masked his feelings beneath a facade of support, choosing to honor the blossoming romance between his companions, even as it tore at the seams of his own desires.

As the seasons turned and the circle of life unfolded, Lakleai and Truzie welcomed two offspring into their midst—Kera, a spirited adventurer, and Honolo, a dutiful caretaker of their humble abode. Their laughter and joy filled the air, a testament to the idyllic existence they had forged amidst the rugged terrain.

Yet, beneath the facade of familial bliss, a simmering resentment festered within Helono's heart, his unrequited love festering like a wound left untended. Envious of the happiness that eluded him, he nursed his grievances in silence, biding his time until fate intervened.

One fateful night, as the moon cast its silvery glow upon the earth, Helono's simmering resentment boiled over into a torrent of jealousy and rage. With a heart heavy with grief and desperation, he seized a jagged rock and plunged it into Truzie's unsuspecting form, extinguishing the light of his rival's life.

In the aftermath of the deed, Helono's hands trembled with guilt and remorse, yet he pressed forward with his macabre charade, concocting a tale of a predatory beast's attack to mask the truth of his betrayal. As Lakleai's tears mingled with the blood-soaked earth, Kera, roused from her slumber by the commotion, stumbled upon the grim tableau, her innocent eyes wide with horror and disbelief.

Unbeknownst to the mortals, the gods watched in silent anguish, their voices unheard amidst the chaos of mortal strife. Annimkamakai, her heart heavy with sorrow, sought to intervene, but found her divine counsel falling on deaf ears, for mortals could not perceive the presence of gods save within the hallowed confines of sacred ground.

Thus, amidst the tangled web of mortal folly and divine indifference, the tragedy of the first Hinkis unfolded—a tale of love unrequited, jealousy unbridled, and the immutable hand of fate guiding humanity's uncertain path.

The First Humans

After countless generations of evolution, the ancient beings known as the Hinkis gradually transformed into modern-day humans. Among the first of these new humans were a trio named Yahweh, Dunnos, and Atricia. Yahweh stood out for his wisdom and adventurous spirit; he often led hunts and consistently returned with the most meat, earning him respect and admiration. Dunnos, on the other hand, was a quiet and reserved individual who stayed close to the huts, dedicating his time to preserving the meat and supporting the trio.

He shared a particularly close bond with Atricia. Atricia herself was a remarkable blend of intelligence and beauty, capable of interpreting animal signals with remarkable speed. Her captivating appearance won the admiration of both Yahweh and Dunnos.

As previously mentioned, the fates of these three would unfold in a manner only slightly less tragic than that of Lakleai, Helono, and Truzie. In time, Atricia revealed her feelings, choosing Dunnos over Yahweh. This revelation shattered Yahweh, who could not bear the thought of Dunnos and Atricia finding happiness together. Consumed by jealousy and rage, Yahweh confronted them one fateful night. In a fit of uncontrollable fury, he stabbed Dunnos multiple times with a dagger he had fashioned from animal bones. Atricia's desperate pleas for him to stop fell on deaf ears.

After ensuring Dunnos was dead, Yahweh turned his attention to Atricia, attempting to win her over through force and intimidation. However, Atricia, despite her fear and grief, stood firm. She told Yahweh that she could never love him the way he loved her. So Yahweh decided to take advantage of her weakness at the time and assaulted her. Atricia begged him to get off of her and leave her alone, but Yahweh was once again deaf to her cries and pleas. Once he was satisfied, he let her go. Atricia was shaken and traumatized from what had just happened.

Once Yahweh fell asleep, Atricia saw her chance and bolted, her heart pounding with fear and adrenaline. She ran through the dense forest, branches scratching her arms and legs, until she reached the river. There, by the water's edge, sat Annimkamakai, her serene presence in the very spot where she had been born, a place now considered Holy ground. The air around this sacred area seemed to shimmer with an ethereal glow, a testament to its divine significance.

Atricia, trembling and breathless, collapsed onto the soft, damp earth, her sobs breaking the tranquil silence. She could hardly process the horrors she had just endured, and tears streamed down her face as she tried to catch her breath. The pain of losing her true love and the fear of Yahweh's wrath replayed in her mind, an unending nightmare she couldn't escape.

Hearing Atricia's anguished cries, Annimkamakai rose gracefully and approached her. The goddess's eyes, filled with empathy and wisdom, met Atricia's tear-filled gaze. "What troubles you, dear child?" she asked softly, her voice like a soothing balm to Atricia's tormented soul.

Through choked sobs, Atricia recounted her tragic tale. She spoke of her true love's untimely death at the hands of Yahweh and the subsequent terror that had driven her to flee. The words tumbled out in a rush, each one laced with grief and desperation. "I was so scared," Atricia whispered, "scared that Yahweh would do it again. I couldn't stay. I had to run."

Annimkamakai listened intently, her expression growing more resolute with each word. When Atricia finished, the goddess gently placed a hand on her shoulder. "You are safe here,"

Annimkamakai assured her. "This is Holy ground, and no harm shall befall you here."

With a deep breath, Annimkamakai made a decision. "I will help you," she declared. "You shall be reborn as a demigoddess. In this new form, you will possess strength and power beyond mortal comprehension. You will be free from Yahweh's reach and anyone else who might seek to harm you. Never again will you suffer as you have. But first, take a sharp rock from this land and stab yourself with it; your blood will shed upon Holy ground and you shall be reborn as the demigoddess Bégán. Once you become a demigoddess, not only will you no longer have to suffer like that again, but if anyone else does, you shall be able to deliver their tears and cries to the gods."

Hope flickered in Atricia's eyes for the first time since her ordeal began. She nodded, her heart swelling with gratitude but also fear and insecurity. Annimkamakai's promise was a beacon of light in her darkest hour, offering her a chance at a new beginning, free from fear and pain. The transformation would mark the end of her suffering and the start of a powerful, new chapter in her existence. She grabbed the rock and stabbed herself through the heart.

As Atricia's blood mingled with the sacred soil, a radiant light enveloped her. Her body transformed, pain giving way to an overwhelming sense of power and clarity. She rose, no longer a mere mortal but the demigoddess Bégán, with a mission to protect others from the pain she had endured. The forest, river, and holy ground bore witness to the birth of a new guardian, destined to bring hope and justice to those in need.

The Ancient Fate

Word of Atricia's fate eventually reached Yahweh's ears, sparking a desire within him to become a demigod, invulnerable to harm. He knew, however, that the same benevolent goddess who had bestowed Atricia with her divine abilities would not grant him the same favor. Determined to achieve his goal by any means necessary, Yahweh scoured ancient maps and sacred texts, searching tirelessly for a place of great spiritual power. After an exhaustive quest, he finally discovered the birthplace of Herika, the goddess herself.

Feigning injury and claiming abandonment by his people, Yahweh fabricated a story of persecution, asserting that his own kin sought his life. Moved by his tale of woe and touched by his seemingly humble demeanor, the compassionate Herika decided to grant Yahweh the same divine powers she had given to Atricia. With his newfound abilities, Yahweh felt a surge of exhilaration and a dark desire to test the limits of his powers.

He began his reign of chaos by overseeing the evolution of the Hinki, guiding their transformation into what would eventually become modern humans. Instead of nurturing them, he chose to torment them. Yahweh unleashed his wrath upon the world, summoning storms that struck with deadly thunderbolts, decimating livestock and ravaging crops. His malicious actions plunged the world into turmoil and despair.

Witnessing the havoc Yahweh wrought, Maheai'ja, another powerful deity, decided that the world could no longer endure his malevolence. In a monumental effort, she initiated the splitting of the world, a process intended not only to promote individuality but also to scatter humanity across the globe, making it harder for Yahweh to manipulate them into ending humanity. This, however, was no swift task. As Maheai'ja worked tirelessly to divide the continents, Yahweh concocted a plan to annihilate humanity.

He poisoned the fruits of a tree with two lethal plagues, ensuring that anyone who consumed them would perish. As Adam and Eve, a couple in search of sustenance, wandered into this holy ground, Yahweh saw his chance. He deceived them, claiming that eating the fruit would grant them eternal life. Trusting his words, for deceit was unknown in the world, they approached the tree.

At that critical moment, Annimkamakai, another deity with a protective heart, intervened. Transforming into a serpent, she slithered close, allowing Adam and Eve to perceive her outside the sacred boundaries. She revealed Yahweh's true intentions, warning them of the deadly consequences. Yahweh, enraged by her interference and now filled with an even deeper hatred for humanity, plotted further destruction.

However, by the time he devised a new scheme, Maheai'ja had completed her task. The world was now separated, its inhabitants scattered. Foiled but not defeated, Yahweh retreated into his thoughts, scheming once more. He envisioned a plan so dark and terrible, one that would require acts of unspeakable cruelty, yet Yahweh, driven by his insatiable thirst for power and control, did not hesitate.

Seeking an ally in his dark endeavors, Yahweh set his sights on Quatica, the goddess of the oceans. He approached her with false charm, attempting to seduce her with flattery and promises of shared power. Quatica, however, was not easily swayed. She saw through Yahweh's deceitful intentions and rejected his advances, demanding that he leave her domain at once. That's when Yahweh's demeanor shifted from manipulative to monstrous. He grabbed Quatica by her wrist with a vice-like grip and threw her violently onto the cold, unyielding floor. Ignoring her cries and desperate pleas, he assaulted her just as he had done to Atricia. Quatica's voice, filled with pain and terror, begged him to stop, but

Yahweh was deaf to her suffering. When he finally relented, a sinister satisfaction gleaming in his eyes, he issued a chilling threat: if she did not flood the entire world, he would subject her to the same horror again.

Quatica, her body trembling and her spirit shattered, stared into Yahweh's cold, merciless eyes. She saw the cruel intent in his gaze and knew he would make good on his threat. With tears streaming down her face and trauma searing her mind, Quatica began the agonizing task of flooding the world. Her divine powers, once a source of life and beauty, now became instruments of destruction.

As the waters rose, covering fields and forests, mountains and valleys, a man named Noah found himself aboard his sturdy boat. By some stroke of fate or divine intervention, his vessel was buoyed by the swelling waves. The same happened for other races scattered across the globe; humanity was, once again, spared from total annihilation, but countless lives were still lost to the relentless floodwaters.

Quatica, her heart heavy with guilt and sorrow, fled to her mother, Maheai'ja. She recounted the nightmarish ordeal, her voice breaking with each word. Maheai'ja listened, her eyes filling with sorrow for her daughter's pain. She wanted nothing more than to avenge Quatica and bring Yahweh to justice. However, with Yahweh now wielding the powers of a god, Maheai'ja found herself powerless to punish him. The balance of divine power prevented her from acting against him directly, leaving her with a deep sense of helplessness and frustration.

Though unable to exact immediate retribution, Maheai'ja vowed to find a way to protect her daughter and ensure that Yahweh's tyranny would one day come to an end. She embraced Quatica, offering her solace and a promise that they would work together to counter Yahweh's malevolence. The tides of divine conflict had been set in motion, and the struggle for justice had only just begun.

The Israeli Fate

The tale of Atricia's fate spread across the Asian and European territories like wildfire, whispered in the marketplaces, and murmured in the quiet corners of villages. Her story was a gripping narrative of divine interaction and human folly, captivating the imagination of all who heard it. However, as time passed and storytellers turned to new tales, Atricia's legend began to fade from memory. The lack of written records hastened its descent into obscurity, until it was nearly forgotten by the world.

In a strange twist of fate, the very obscurity of Atricia's tale sparked a peculiar trend among the people. Inspired by her story, they began to mimic her actions, seeking favor from the gods. Yet, the gods had grown wiser and more discerning. They no longer tolerated such naive gestures. These acts of devotion, born out of a long-forgotten myth, led many to their deaths without divine intervention or reward. As the story was forgotten, so too were the reasons behind these tragic sacrifices.

With Atricia's tale relegated to myth, people began to worship false gods, creating new deities to fill the void left by the old ones. This shift in belief was both a concern and a non-issue for the gods. While most civilizations moved on with their new pantheon, one group in particular drew the attention of the gods: the Israelites.

The Israelites maintained that Atricia's story was true, holding fast to the belief that Yahweh, their god, had been justified in his actions. Yet, aware that their views were controversial, they formed a secretive cult under the leadership of a man named Abraham. This group aimed to spread their interpretation of the tale among their people, fostering a community rooted in their unique faith.

Feai'ka, one of the ancient gods, decided to punish the Israelites for their defiance and their worship of what he saw as a false god. He decreed a harsh fate for them: they would be conquered repeatedly, driven from their homes, persecuted for their beliefs, and subjected to endless suffering. This divine retribution manifested in the long history of hardship faced by the Jewish people.

However, the great mother Maheai'ja, a deity of compassion and forgiveness, intervened on behalf of the Israelites. She persuaded Feai'ka to promise that one day, the Jewish people would be redeemed. Their suffering would not be eternal. She envisioned a future where they would live in prosperity and peace, their hardships forgotten.

Maheai'ja's vision for the Israelites was one of a Utopian existence. She imagined a land akin to the mythical Aluminak, where flowers bloomed in perpetual beauty, and crops were always abundant. In this paradise, animals would willingly offer their gifts and sacrifices to humans in exchange for protection, creating a harmonious balance between all living beings. It was a world where every human desire and need would be fulfilled, a land of luxury, hope, and gentleness.

In this promised future, the Jewish people would finally have their eyes opened to the truth and live a life free from suffering. Their journey would be one from persecution to prosperity, a testament to the enduring spirit of their faith and the eventual mercy of the gods.

The Ancient Fate

Soon, Yahweh's fabricated and sugarcoated story began to spread far and wide. This revised narrative completely erased Atricia and Dunnos from history, portraying Yahweh as a divine being who had been born and created as a god. He was depicted as a benevolent father figure who smiled upon his children and granted their prayers. This false image of Yahweh as a kind and omnipotent deity boosted his confidence. He believed that as long as people continued to believe in and worship him, he could get away with any atrocity he desired.

Emboldened by his growing number of followers, Yahweh created two places: Heaven and Hell, mimicking the paradisiacal Aluminak and the torturous Hekkinak. He demanded unwavering worship from his followers, threatening them with eternal damnation in Hell if they disobeyed. Those who were kind-hearted but did not believe in Yahweh were condemned to Hell, while some wicked individuals who professed their faith in him were rewarded with Heaven. This blatant unfairness was largely ignored by the masses, who were too fearful to question Yahweh's authority. Those who dared to question or criticize him faced severe punishment, either from Yahweh himself or from his fervent followers.

Under Yahweh's tyrannical rule, the world descended into chaos. Wars raged unchecked, diseases spread like wildfire, crops withered and died, and natural disasters became increasingly frequent. Yahweh cared little for the suffering of humanity, as long as they continued to worship him and meet his demands. His capricious nature and disregard for justice caused immense pain and turmoil, but the people remained subservient out of fear of his wrath.

Yahweh's confidence grew, leading him to once again approach Quatica with the intent to assault her. This time, his motivation was pure gratification. Quatica, horrified, attempted to escape into the waters, the one place Yahweh dared not tread. But Yahweh, filled with ruthless determination, pulled her out of the water and violated her. Despite her desperate pleas for him to stop, Yahweh was relentless. After he was satisfied, he threatened Quatica into silence, fearing retribution from the other gods.

Quatica, traumatized and terrified, kept her silence. However, it soon became apparent that she was pregnant. Annimkamakai, noticing the change, confronted Quatica about how she had become pregnant. Overwhelmed with emotion, Quatica tearfully recounted the horrific assault.

Annimkamakai was filled with an overwhelming rage and hatred towards Yahweh. Despite Yahweh's status as a demigod, which protected him from direct retribution from other gods, Annimkamakai was determined to deliver justice. She had witnessed Yahweh's countless atrocities, not just against Quatica and Atricia, but against many others. His willingness to let wars rage and suffering spread for his own sake fueled her anger.

In her fury, Annimkamakai decided to break the most sacred rule among the gods: to never punish the innocent for the crimes of the guilty. She orchestrated a plan to bring Yahweh to justice by unleashing a deadly plague. She had rats eat from the same tree that was intended to end humanity, and then spread the plague into Europe. The pestilence spread rapidly, decimating populations and causing immense suffering.

The plague soon spilled over into Asia, beyond Annimkamakai's initial intentions, and there was nothing she could do to halt its spread. As people succumbed to the plague in vast numbers, they began to question Yahweh's divinity and his supposed benevolence. Their faith in him waned, significantly weakening his power.

Filled with rage over his diminishing power, Yahweh attempted to retaliate against Annimkamakai. However, she was prepared for his wrath. Transforming into a snake, she struck him with a venomous bite, injecting a paralyzing venom into his veins. This venom did not kill Yahweh but left him in constant, excruciating pain for several years.

Tyrant's heritage (not a real story)

There was once a land filled with berries, fruits, beauty, and animals which the Elven people lived. Elven people had brownish-orange skin, pointy ears and white hair. Their land was a paradise, nobody could ever want to live somewhere else. However, one day the king of Andalore, who was the Elven goddess' son decided that the elves should be slaves for humans. So he sent two armadas out to go and capture Elves and deliver them into slavery.

The men reached the shores of the elven land and the elves welcomed the men with open arms and even some gifts. The men then started attacking them, throwing fire everywhere, burning their homes down, threatening them to get into the boats, and shooting those who tried to escape. The elves had no choice but to do what they said. However the elves had faith, they believed that soon their goddess would do something about their enslavement and would one day walk the same soil of their ancestral land.

The king soon built them a village with very little budget and only one hut looked the different. The king believed that the elves hadn't worked hard enough to earn such rich materials for their housing, unlike the humans or at least some of the humans for the humans who believed that what the king was doing was wrong were punished by being enslaved alongside the elves. What's even worse is that the king made it a tradition that once a year the humans could raid the elven town for any goods and if anyone were to try and stop them they'd be punished severely. One day, however, during another human raid, a mother was desperately trying to save her daughter from the cruelty of humans when she tripped. She was then chased away by some nearby humans.

The child then fell upon the steps of a temple for the elven goddess. A priestess named Quata found the child and decided to deliver them out of slavery. So she ran towards the river through the streets filled with endless chaos then made her way into the trading post where she grabbed a basket and placed the child in it. She then sang the child a lullaby to and let it drift off to sleep. She then placed a lid on top of the basket and sent the child drifting off to decide it's fate. The Elven goddess, watching this decided to ask one of her daughters, who was the goddess of water to ensure that the child would have a safe passage to the castle. She made her way through the water and into the old royal bathing quarters which the royals now used to swim. The queen had just finished teaching her son, Johnathon, currently four years of age how to swim.

The queen wore her bathing outfit which was just a corset and a small skirt on top meanwhile

One of the servants, took a glance behind her to watch the beautiful sunset for just a moment. She then glanced at the brown, flaky, almost beat up basket from the harsh and long journey, she then touched the basket which felt hard and itchy. She slowly lifted up the lid from the basket, wondering where her handmaid was, the queen turned around and saw her servant lifting up the lid from the basket. The queen rushed over to take a peak at what her handmaid was looking at.

The Handmaid lifted the lid from the basket and revealed the elven child. The sun was just at the right spot that it's light bounced off her hair making it seem like her hair was made out of moonlight and her eyes, like emeralds sparkled as they looked into the eyes of the handmaid. Soon believing that fate had brought this baby to them, they decided that fate was not to be ignored and accepted the gift. The handmaid raised the child as her own and named her Kera.

Kera spent her days in the castle, sweeping and mopping the floors, and being at the side of Prince Johnathon, which she felt more like a friend to him than a servant. They both played together when they were young, she helped pick out outfits for him, comforted him whenever he needed it the most, and was all together with him for most hours of the day alongside her best friend Selena, who was another elf that was delivered out of slavery and into the castle.

Selena was a beautiful elven girl who always wore her hair up in a braid. She constantly accompanied Kera and Johnathon. She was kind and caring and always supportive to everyone when they needed it the most. Her white hair always glowed like moonlight every time light ever reflected upon it. and her eyes, a crystal clear gray as can be.

One day, the king Joseph and Queen Marilyn decided that it was time for their son to take the throne and wear the crown. Johnathon was extremely honored by their decision to make him king. He had always dreamed of the day when a crown would sit atop his brownish orange hair, and that his eyes which were the absolute most perfect shade of brown would meet the eyes of the people celebrating his coronation.

Johnathon wanted his coronation to be special, so he went up to his father and proposed that there be a grand feast at his coronation where both the nobility and the peasants can enjoy a party filled with joy, music, laughter, dance, the smell of fun and food, and wine everywhere. His father decided to accept the request.

Johnathon was then about to exit the throne room which had the most beautiful red carpet leading up to the the king's throne which contained skulls from his enemies that he had already defeated. The gold trim of the carpet had a natural glow but with the sunlight from the medium sized windows did it look like magic.

"My son, there is also something else that I must discuss with you" Joseph announced.

"What is it?" Johnathon asked.

"A king must always be accompanied by a wife, meaning that soon after this feast you will have to choose one." Joseph told him.

"I know," said Johnathon, "and I've already chosen her." "Have you?" Joseph asked.

"Yes, I've already invited her and I plan to propose to her at the feast." Johnathon confirmed to Joseph.

"Well I look forward to seeing who you have chosen to be your queen." Joseph replied.

"You may not think highly of her at first but I can assure you I know exactly what I am doing." Johnathon said.

Meanwhile, Kera and Selena were trying to figure out what to wear to the feast. The fanciest dress Kera owned was the dress that female servants wore whenever they were working at a party that the royals threw. Selena comforted her by saying that the dress was acceptable. Kera sighed and decided to tell her what she was really worried about.

"The entire kingdom will be there, what if they don't like me because I'm an elf?" Selena smiled and directed Kera's attention to the mirror. She then announced;

"With a face and body that pretty I don't think they'll even care if your elven or not"

Kera smiled.

Soon a servant arrived acknowledging that prince Johnathon had ordered a dress for Kera to wear to the feast. It was a beautiful white dress with bright pink corset, pearls trimming almost every part of it, and it even had a golden trim to the light pink corset. Kera, excited, immediately tried it on with the help of Selena. A few hours later, the feast finally began Selena and Kera left the servant's quarters and made their way down the staircase lit by the moon's light from the glass roof and into the banquet hall.

All sorts of people were there, it is just like how prince Johnathon had planned it, the Nobility and the poor finally getting along with each other and finally having a good time. Soon, the dance began. Johnathon asked Kera if she'd like to dance with him. Kera nodded her head and they both made their way to the dance floor.

Joseph and Marilyn were watching them from their table. They knew that Kera was most likely to be a slave before she was delivered into the castle. They feared that with a former slave in charge slavery would be destroyed and abolished. But they assumed that it was just a dance and that Kera wasn't actually the one he was going to propose to.

Soon, the time was right. Johnathon ordered the dance floor to be clear so that it was just him and Kera. They both danced together for a few minutes. Then Johnathon pulled out a ring and asked Kera to be his. Kera didn't know much about marriage so she told him that she'd have to do more research before she accepted or denied his proposal Johnathon agreed.

After the feast, Selena and Kera decided to sneak into the elven village out of pure curiosity Selena was against it, she believed that the other elves were untamed savages and that's why they're enslaved since they had to be kept away from the people. However Kera's curiosity got the best of her and she snuck in anyways.

She then bumped into the same priestess that had previously saved her life from the humans. The priestess explained how she had just barely heard a year ago what fate Kera ended up with. She was overjoyed to know that Kera was okay. Kera, confused began to ask her more questions when another human raid took place. Everyone began screaming, yelling, and running all over the place like mice being chased by cats Kera was horrified by what she was seeing, her own people being attacked and slaughtered before her very eyes.

Once she made it back to the castle she confronted Johnathon about these issues expecting him to do something about it. But

Johnathan then began to justify it. Since Johnathon wouldn't listen Kera decided not to marry him. Johnathon then got strict. He deemed that Kera wouldn't have a choice in the matter anymore and that they would be wedded tomorrow in the afternoon. He ordered his guards to lock Kera up with no food or water until then. Kera sobbing decided to pray to the elven goddess about this. That's all the elves ever had to do was pray. Kera's prayer was soon answered and all sorts of natural disasters occurred after that. Destroying the kingdom of Andalore. Soon not only was Kera now free from marriage but the slaves were also free now. Kera remembered all the good times she had spent with Johnathon but now

she had to move on. They rode on the same two
armadas that had previously enslaved them
and they rode it back home where they'd be
free.

* 9 7 9 8 2 2 7 7 4 3 2 9 9 *